Contents

In the Soup

Fiesta Black Bean Soup

Slow Cooker Recipe

6 cups chicken broth
1 can (16 ounces) black beans, drained
¾ pound potatoes, peeled and diced
½ pound ham, diced
½ onion, diced
1 can (4 ounces) chopped jalapeño peppers
2 cloves garlic, minced
2 teaspoons dried oregano leaves
1½ teaspoons dried thyme leaves
1 teaspoon ground cumin
    Sour cream, chopped bell peppers and chopped tomatoes
        for garnish

Combine all ingredients, except garnish, in slow cooker. Cover and cook on Low 8 to 10 hours or on High 4 to 5 hours. Garnish, if desired.   *Makes 6 to 8 servings*

Fiesta Black Bean Soup

Potato and Leek Soup

Slow Cooker Recipe

4 cups chicken broth
3 potatoes, peeled and diced
1½ cups chopped cabbage
1 leek, diced
1 onion, chopped
2 carrots, diced
¼ cup chopped parsley
2 teaspoons salt
2 teaspoons black pepper
½ teaspoon caraway seeds
1 bay leaf
½ cup sour cream
1 pound bacon, cooked and crumbled

Combine chicken broth, potatoes, cabbage, leek, onion, carrots and parsley in large bowl; pour mixture into slow cooker. Stir in salt, pepper, caraway seeds and bay leaf. Cover and cook on Low 8 to 10 hours or on High 4 to 5 hours. Remove and discard bay leaf. Combine some hot liquid from slow cooker with sour cream in small bowl. Add mixture to slow cooker; stir. Stir in bacon.

Makes 6 to 8 servings

Potato and Leek Soup

Ranch Clam Chowder

¼ cup chopped onion
3 tablespoons butter or margarine
½ pound fresh mushrooms, sliced
2 tablespoons Worcestershire sauce
1½ cups half-and-half
1 can (10¾ ounces) cream of potato soup
¼ cup dry white wine
1 package (1 ounce) HIDDEN VALLEY® Milk Recipe Original
    Ranch® Salad Dressing Mix
1 can (10 ounces) whole baby clams, undrained
    Chopped parsley

In 3-quart saucepan, cook onion in butter over medium heat until onion is soft but not browned. Add mushrooms and Worcestershire sauce. Cook until mushrooms are soft and pan juices have almost evaporated. In medium bowl, whisk together half-and-half, potato soup, wine and salad dressing mix until smooth. Drain clam liquid into dressing mixture; stir into mushrooms in pan. Cook, uncovered, until soup is heated through but not boiling. Add clams to soup; cook until heated through. Garnish each serving with parsley.

Makes 6 servings

Ranch Clam Chowder

Vegetable Medley Soup

Slow Cooker Recipe

3 sweet potatoes, peeled and chopped
3 zucchini, chopped
2 cups chopped broccoli
1 onion, chopped
¼ cup butter, melted
3 cans (about 14 ounces each) chicken broth
2 white potatoes, peeled and shredded
1 rib celery, finely chopped
1 tablespoon salt
1 teaspoon ground cumin
1 teaspoon black pepper
2 cups half-and-half or milk

Combine sweet potatoes, zucchini, broccoli, onion and butter in large bowl. Add chicken broth; stir. Add white potatoes, celery, salt, cumin and pepper; stir. Pour mixture into slow cooker. Cover and cook on Low 8 to 10 hours or on High 4 to 5 hours. Add half-and-half; cook 30 minutes to 1 hour. *Makes 12 servings*

Food Fact: *As with conventional cooking recipes, slow cooker recipe time ranges are provided to account for variables such as temperature of ingredients before cooking, how full the slow cooker is and even altitude. Once you become familiar with your slow cooker, you'll have a good idea which end of the range to use.*

Vegetable Medley Soup

Swanson® Chicken Noodle Soup Express

2 cans (14½ ounces *each*) SWANSON® Chicken Broth
  Generous dash pepper
1 medium carrot, sliced (about ½ cup)
1 stalk celery, sliced (about ½ cup)
½ cup *uncooked* medium egg noodles
1 can (5 ounces) SWANSON® Premium Chunk Chicken Breast
  or Chunk Chicken, drained

In medium saucepan mix broth, pepper, carrot and celery. Over medium-high heat, heat to a boil. Stir in noodles. Reduce heat to medium. Cook 10 minutes, stirring often. Add chicken and heat through. *Makes 4 servings*

Swanson® Easy Vegetable Soup

2 cans (14½ ounces *each*) SWANSON® Chicken Broth
3 cups CAMPBELL'S® Tomato Juice
1 teaspoon dried oregano leaves *or* Italian seasoning, crushed
½ teaspoon garlic powder *or* 4 cloves garlic, minced
¼ teaspoon pepper
1 bag (16 ounces) frozen vegetable combination (broccoli,
  cauliflower, carrots)
1 can (about 15 ounces) kidney beans *or* 1 can (about
  16 ounces) white kidney (cannellini) beans, rinsed and
  drained

In large saucepan mix broth, tomato juice, oregano, garlic powder, pepper and vegetables. Over medium-high heat, heat to a boil. Cover and cook 10 minutes or until vegetables are tender. Add beans and heat through. *Makes 8 servings*

**Top to bottom: Swanson® Easy Vegetable Soup and
Swanson® Chicken Noodle Soup Express**

Tomato Chicken Gumbo

6 chicken thighs
½ pound hot sausage links or Polish sausage, sliced
3 cups water
1 can (14 ounces) chicken broth
½ cup uncooked long-grain white rice
1 can (26 ounces) DEL MONTE® Traditional or Chunky Garlic
    and Herb Spaghetti Sauce
1 can (11 ounces) DEL MONTE® SUMMER CRISP™ Whole
    Kernel Golden Sweet Corn, drained
1 medium green bell pepper, diced

1. Preheat oven to 400°F. In large shallow baking pan, place chicken and sausage. Bake 35 minutes or until chicken is no longer pink in center. Cool slightly.

2. Remove skin from chicken; cut meat into cubes. Cut sausage into slices ½ inch thick.

3. In 6-quart pot, bring water and broth to a boil. Add chicken, sausage and rice. Cover; cook over medium heat 15 minutes.

4. Stir in spaghetti sauce, corn and bell pepper; bring to a boil. Cover; cook 5 minutes or until rice is tender.   *Makes 4 servings*

Tip: Add additional water or broth for a thinner gumbo. For spicier gumbo, serve with hot red pepper sauce.

Tomato Chicken Gumbo

Slews of Stews

The Best Beef Stew

Slow Cooker Recipe

½ cup plus 2 tablespoons all-purpose flour, divided
2 teaspoons salt
1 teaspoon black pepper
3 pounds beef stew meat, trimmed and cut into cubes
1 can (16 ounces) diced tomatoes in juice, undrained
½ pound smoked sausage, sliced
3 potatoes, peeled and diced
1 cup chopped leek
1 cup chopped onion
4 ribs celery, sliced
½ cup chicken broth
3 cloves garlic, minced
1 teaspoon dried thyme leaves
3 tablespoons water

Combine ½ cup flour, salt and pepper in resealable plastic food storage bag. Add beef; shake bag to coat beef. Place beef in slow cooker. Add remaining ingredients except remaining 2 tablespoons flour and water; stir well. Cover and cook on Low 8 to 12 hours or on High 4 to 6 hours. One hour before serving, turn slow cooker to High. Combine remaining 2 tablespoons flour and water in small bowl. Stir mixture into slow cooker; mix well. Cover and cook until thickened. *Makes 8 servings*

The Best Beef Stew

Turkey Mushroom Stew

Slow Cooker Recipe

1 pound turkey cutlets, cut into 4×1-inch
strips
1 small yellow onion, thinly sliced
2 tablespoons minced green onions with tops
½ pound mushrooms, sliced
2 to 3 tablespoons flour
1 cup half-and-half or milk
1 teaspoon dried tarragon leaves
1 teaspoon salt
Black pepper to taste
½ cup frozen peas
½ cup sour cream (optional)
Puff pastry shells

Layer turkey, onions and mushrooms in slow cooker. Cover and cook on Low 4 hours. Remove turkey and vegetables to serving bowl. Turn slow cooker to High.

Blend flour into half-and-half until smooth; pour into slow cooker. Add tarragon, salt and pepper to slow cooker. Return cooked vegetables and turkey to slow cooker. Stir in peas. Cover and cook 1 hour or until sauce has thickened and peas are heated through.

Stir in sour cream just before serving, if desired. Serve in puff pastry shells. *Makes 4 servings*

Turkey Mushroom Stew

Spicy Sichuan Pork Stew

2 pounds boneless pork shoulder (Boston butt)
¼ cup all-purpose flour
2 tablespoons vegetable oil
1¾ cups water, divided
¼ cup KIKKOMAN® Soy Sauce
3 tablespoons dry sherry
2 cloves garlic, pressed
1 teaspoon minced fresh ginger root
½ teaspoon crushed red pepper
¼ teaspoon fennel seed, crushed
8 green onions and tops, cut into 1-inch lengths, separating
     whites from tops
2 large carrots, cut into chunks
   Hot cooked rice

Cut pork into 1-inch cubes. Coat in flour; reserve 2 tablespoons remaining flour. Heat oil in Dutch oven or large pan over medium-high heat; brown pork on all sides in hot oil. Add 1½ cups water, soy sauce, sherry, garlic, ginger, red pepper, fennel seed and white parts of green onions. Cover pan; bring to boil. Reduce heat and simmer 30 minutes. Add carrots; simmer, covered, 30 minutes longer, or until pork and carrots are tender. Meanwhile, combine reserved flour and remaining ¼ cup water; set aside. Stir green onion tops into pork mixture; simmer 1 minute. Add flour mixture; bring to boil. Cook and stir until mixture is slightly thickened. Serve with rice.   *Makes 6 servings*

Spicy Sichuan Pork Stew

Stewed Catfish and Bell Peppers

1½ pounds catfish fillets or other firm white-fleshed fish
1 onion, chopped
1 *each* green and red bell pepper, cut into 1-inch pieces
1 clove garlic, minced
1 cup clam juice
1 tomato, chopped
¼ cup FRANK'S® REDHOT® Sauce
2 tablespoons minced parsley

1. On sheet of waxed paper, mix *2 tablespoons flour* with *½ teaspoon salt*. Lightly coat fillets with flour mixture; set aside.

2. Heat *1 tablespoon oil* in large nonstick skillet until hot. Add onion, bell peppers and garlic. Cook and stir 3 minutes or until crisp-tender; transfer to dish.

3. Heat *1 tablespoon oil* in same skillet until hot. Cook fillets 5 minutes or until golden brown, turning once. Return vegetables to skillet. Add clam juice, tomato, REDHOT sauce and parsley. Heat to boiling. Reduce heat to medium-low. Cook, covered, 8 to 10 minutes or until fish flakes with fork. Serve with hot cooked rice, if desired.

Makes 6 servings

Stewed Catfish and Bell Peppers

Santa Fe Stew Olé

1 tablespoon vegetable oil
1½ pounds beef stew meat, cut into bite-size pieces
1 can (28 ounces) stewed tomatoes, undrained
2 medium carrots, cut into ¼-inch slices
1 medium onion, coarsely chopped
2 tablespoons diced green chiles
1 package (1.0 ounce) LAWRY'S® Taco Spices & Seasonings
½ teaspoon LAWRY'S® Seasoned Salt
¼ cup water
2 tablespoons all-purpose flour
1 can (15 ounces) pinto beans, drained

In Dutch oven, heat oil. Brown stew meat over medium-high heat. Add tomatoes, carrots, onion, green chiles, Taco Spices & Seasonings and Seasoned Salt; mix well. Bring to a boil over medium-high heat; reduce heat to low and cook, covered, 40 minutes. In small bowl, combine water and flour; mix well. Stir into stew mixture. Add pinto beans; cook over low heat 15 minutes. *Makes 4 servings*

Serving Suggestion: Serve with lots of warm corn and flour tortillas.

Santa Fe Stew Olé

Deviled Beef Short Rib Stew

Slow Cooker Recipe

4 pounds beef short ribs, trimmed
2 pounds small red potatoes, scrubbed
   and scored
8 carrots, peeled and cut into chunks
2 onions, cut into thick wedges
1 bottle (12 ounces) beer or non-alcoholic malt beverage
8 tablespoons FRENCH'S® Deli Brown Mustard, divided
3 tablespoons FRENCH'S® Worcestershire Sauce, divided
2 tablespoons cornstarch

1. Broil ribs 6 inches from heat on rack in broiler pan 10 minutes or until well-browned, turning once. Place potatoes, carrots and onions in bottom of slow cooker. Place ribs on top of vegetables.

2. Combine beer, *6 tablespoons* mustard and *2 tablespoons* Worcestershire. Pour into slow cooker. Cover and cook on high-heat setting 5 hours* or until meat is tender.

3. Transfer meat and vegetables to platter; keep warm. Strain fat from broth; pour into saucepan. Combine cornstarch with *2 tablespoons cold water.* Stir into broth with remaining *2 tablespoons* mustard and *1 tablespoon* Worcestershire. Heat to boiling. Reduce heat to medium-low. Cook 1 to 2 minutes or until thickened, stirring often. Pass gravy with meat and vegetables. Serve meat with additional mustard. *Makes 6 servings (with 3 cups gravy)*

*Or cook 10 hours on low-heat setting.

Deviled Beef Short Rib Stew

Stew Provençal

Slow Cooker Recipe

2 cans (about 14 ounces each) beef broth, divided
⅓ cup all-purpose flour
1½ pounds pork tenderloin, trimmed and diced
4 red potatoes, unpeeled, cut into cubes
2 cups frozen cut green beans
1 onion, chopped
2 cloves garlic, minced
1 teaspoon salt
1 teaspoon dried thyme leaves
½ teaspoon black pepper

Combine ¾ cup beef broth and flour in small bowl. Set aside.

Add remaining broth, pork, potatoes, beans, onion, garlic, salt, thyme and pepper to slow cooker; stir. Cover and cook on Low 8 to 10 hours or on High 4 to 5 hours. If cooking on Low, turn to High last 30 minutes. Stir in flour mixture. Cook 30 minutes to thicken.

Makes 8 servings

Food Fact: *You can easily remove most of the fat from accumulated juices, soups and canned broths. The simplest way is to refrigerate the liquid for several hours or overnight. The fat will congeal and float to the top for easy removal.*

Stew Provençal

Vegetable Stew Medley

2 tablespoons CRISCO® Vegetable Oil
4 medium onions, thinly sliced and separated into rings
3 medium green bell peppers, cut into strips
2 cloves garlic, minced
4 medium zucchini, cut into ½-inch pieces
1 medium eggplant, cut into ½-inch pieces (about 1 pound)
1 can (14½ ounces) no-salt-added whole tomatoes, drained and chopped, *or* 4 or 5 fresh tomatoes, peeled and quartered
1 teaspoon dried dill weed
¾ teaspoon dried basil leaves
½ teaspoon dried oregano leaves
½ teaspoon black pepper
¼ teaspoon salt
1 package (9 ounces) frozen peas
¼ cup lemon juice
2 tablespoons chopped fresh parsley *or* 2 teaspoons dried parsley

---

1. Heat oil in Dutch oven (non-reactive or non-cast iron) on medium heat. Add onions, bell peppers and garlic. Cook and stir until tender.

2. Add zucchini and eggplant. Cook 5 minutes, stirring occasionally. Stir in tomatoes, dill weed, basil, oregano, black pepper and salt. Reduce heat to low. Cover. Simmer 20 minutes, stirring occasionally.

3. Stir in peas. Simmer 3 to 5 minutes or until peas are thawed and heated, stirring occasionally. Stir in lemon juice. Serve hot or chilled, sprinkled with parsley. *Makes 12 servings*

Vegetable Stew Medley

Hearty Ground Beef Stew

1 pound ground beef
3 cloves garlic, minced
1 package (16 ounces) Italian-style frozen vegetables
2 cups southern-style hash brown potatoes
1 jar (14 ounces) marinara sauce
1 can (10½ ounces) condensed beef broth
3 tablespoons FRENCH'S® Worcestershire Sauce

1. Brown beef with garlic in large saucepan; drain. Add remaining ingredients. Heat to boiling. Cover. Reduce heat to medium-low. Cook 10 minutes or until vegetables are crisp-tender.

2. Serve in warm bowls with garlic bread, if desired.

Makes 6 servings

Hearty Ground Beef Stew

It's Chili Tonight

Bandstand Chili

---

1 tablespoon vegetable oil
1½ cups chopped onions
1½ cups chopped red bell peppers
2 tablespoons mild Mexican seasoning*
1 clove garlic, minced
1 can (28 ounces) tomato purée with tomato bits
1 can (15½ ounces) light red kidney beans, undrained
2 cups chopped cooked BUTTERBALL® Boneless Young Turkey

---

*To make your own Mexican seasoning, combine 1 tablespoon chili powder, 1½ teaspoons oregano and 1½ teaspoons cumin.

Heat oil in large skillet over medium heat until hot. Add onions, bell peppers, Mexican seasoning and garlic. Cook and stir 4 to 5 minutes. Add tomato purée and beans; stir in turkey. Reduce heat to low; simmer 5 minutes. *Makes 8 servings*

Bandstand Chili

Scrumptious SPAM™ Spring Chili

Nonstick cooking spray
4 cloves garlic, minced
2 green bell peppers, cut into strips
3 (4.25-ounce) jars CHI-CHI'S® Diced Green Chilies
1 cup sliced green onions
2 jalapeño peppers, seeded and minced
2 teaspoons dried oregano leaves
2 teaspoons ground cumin
2 (15-ounce) cans cannellini beans or kidney beans, rinsed
　　and drained
2 (10¾-ounce) cans condensed chicken broth, undiluted
1 (12-ounce) can SPAM® Luncheon Meat, cubed

In large saucepan coated with cooking spray, sauté garlic over medium heat 1 minute. Add bell peppers, chilies, green onions, jalapeños, oregano and cumin; sauté 5 minutes. Stir in beans and broth. Bring to a boil. Cover. Reduce heat and simmer 10 minutes. Stir in SPAM®. Simmer 2 minutes. *Makes 4 to 6 servings*

Vegetable-Beef Chili

1 (1-pound) beef top round or chuck steak, cut into ¼-inch
    cubes
1 tablespoon vegetable oil
1 cup coarsely chopped green bell pepper
½ cup coarsely chopped onion
1 clove garlic, minced
3 to 4 tablespoons chili powder
2 (16-ounce) cans tomatoes, undrained, coarsely chopped
¾ cup A.1.® Original or A.1.® Bold & Spicy Steak Sauce
1 (17-ounce) can corn, drained
1 (15-ounce) can kidney beans, drained

In 6-quart pot, over medium-high heat, brown steak in oil; drain if
necessary. Reduce heat to medium; add pepper, onion and garlic.
Cook and stir until vegetables are tender, about 3 minutes. Mix in
chili powder; cook and stir 1 minute. Add tomatoes with liquid and
steak sauce; heat to a boil. Reduce heat. Cover; simmer 45 minutes,
stirring occasionally. Add corn and beans; simmer 15 minutes or
until steak is tender. Serve immediately. Garnish as desired.

Makes 6 servings

Vegetable-Beef Chili

Chili with Beans and Corn

Slow Cooker Recipe

1 (16-ounce) can black-eyed peas or
  cannellini beans, rinsed and drained
1 (16-ounce) can kidney or navy beans, rinsed
  and drained
1 (15-ounce) can whole tomatoes, drained and chopped
1 onion, chopped
1 cup corn
1 cup water
½ cup chopped green onions
½ cup tomato paste
¼ cup diced canned jalapeño peppers
1 tablespoon chili powder
1 teaspoon mustard
1 teaspoon ground cumin
½ teaspoon dried oregano leaves

Combine all ingredients in slow cooker. Cover and cook on Low 8
to 10 hours or on High 4 to 5 hours.   *Makes 6 to 8 servings*

Food Fact: *Keep a lid on it! The slow cooker can take as long as
twenty minutes to regain the heat lost when the cover is removed. If
the recipe calls for stirring or checking the dish near the end of the
cooking time, replace the lid as quickly as you can.*

Chili with Beans and Corn

Meaty Chili

1 pound coarsely ground beef
¼ pound ground Italian sausage
1 large onion, chopped
2 medium ribs celery, diced
2 fresh jalapeño peppers,* chopped
2 cloves garlic, minced
1 can (28 ounces) whole peeled tomatoes, undrained, cut up
1 can (15 ounces) pinto beans, drained
1 can (12 ounces) tomato juice
1 cup water
¼ cup ketchup
1 teaspoon sugar
1 teaspoon chili powder
½ teaspoon salt
½ teaspoon ground cumin
½ teaspoon dried thyme leaves
⅛ teaspoon black pepper

*Jalapeño peppers can sting and irritate the skin; wear rubber gloves when handling peppers and do not touch eyes.

Cook beef, sausage, onion, celery, jalapeños and garlic in 5-quart Dutch oven over medium-high heat until meat is browned and onion is tender, stirring frequently.

Stir in tomatoes with liquid, beans, tomato juice, water, ketchup, sugar, chili powder, salt, cumin, thyme and black pepper. Bring to a boil over high heat. Reduce heat to medium-low; simmer, uncovered, 30 minutes, stirring occasionally.

Ladle into bowls. Garnish, if desired. *Makes 6 servings*

Vegetable Chili

2 cans (15 ounces each) chunky chili tomato sauce
1 bag (16 ounces) BIRDS EYE® frozen Farm Fresh Mixtures
    Broccoli, Corn and Red Peppers
1 can (15½ ounces) red kidney beans, rinsed and drained
1 can (4½ ounces) chopped green chilies
½ cup shredded Cheddar cheese

• Combine tomato sauce, vegetables, beans and chilies in large saucepan; bring to boil.

• Cook, uncovered, over medium heat 5 minutes.

• Sprinkle individual servings with cheese.   *Makes 4 to 6 servings*

Vegetable Chili

Main Dish Magic

Simple Coq au Vin

Slow Cooker Recipe

4 chicken legs
  Salt and black pepper
2 tablespoons olive oil
½ pound mushrooms, sliced
1 onion, sliced into rings
½ cup red wine
½ teaspoon dried basil leaves
½ teaspoon dried thyme leaves
½ teaspoon dried oregano leaves
  Hot cooked rice

Sprinkle chicken with salt and pepper. Heat oil in large skillet; brown chicken on both sides. Remove chicken and place in slow cooker. Sauté mushrooms and onion in same skillet. Add wine; stir and scrape brown bits from bottom of skillet. Add mixture to slow cooker. Sprinkle with basil, thyme and oregano. Cover and cook on Low 8 to 10 hours or on High 3 to 4 hours.

Serve chicken and sauce over rice. *Makes 4 servings*

Simple Coq au Vin

Broccoli and Beef Pasta

Slow Cooker Recipe

2 cups broccoli florets *or* 1 package
   (10 ounces) frozen broccoli, thawed
1 onion, thinly sliced
½ teaspoon dried basil leaves
½ teaspoon dried oregano leaves
½ teaspoon dried thyme leaves
1 can (14½ ounces) Italian-style diced tomatoes, undrained
¾ cup beef broth
1 pound lean ground beef
2 cloves garlic, minced
2 tablespoons tomato paste
2 cups cooked rotini pasta
3 ounces shredded Cheddar cheese or grated Parmesan
   cheese

Layer broccoli, onion, basil, oregano, thyme, tomatoes and broth in slow cooker. Cover and cook on Low 2½ hours.

Combine beef and garlic in large nonstick skillet; cook over high heat 6 to 8 minutes or until meat is no longer pink, breaking meat apart with wooden spoon. Pour off drippings. Add beef mixture to slow cooker. Cover and cook 2 hours.

Stir in tomato paste. Add pasta and cheese. Cover and cook 30 minutes or until cheese melts and mixture is heated through.

Makes 4 servings

Broccoli and Beef Pasta

Barbara's Pork Chop Dinner

Slow Cooker Recipe

1 tablespoon butter
1 tablespoon olive oil
6 bone-in pork loin chops
1 can (10¾ ounces) condensed cream of chicken soup, undiluted
1 can (4 ounces) mushrooms, drained and chopped
¼ cup Dijon mustard
¼ cup chicken broth
2 cloves garlic, minced
½ teaspoon salt
½ teaspoon dried basil leaves
¼ teaspoon black pepper
6 red potatoes, unpeeled, cut into thin slices
1 onion, sliced
Chopped parsley

Heat butter and oil in large skillet. Brown pork chops on both sides. Set aside.

Combine soup, mushrooms, mustard, chicken broth, garlic, salt, basil and pepper in slow cooker. Add potatoes and onion, stirring to coat. Place pork chops on top of potato mixture. Cover and cook on Low 8 to 10 hours or on High 4 to 5 hours. Sprinkle with parsley.

Makes 6 servings

Barbara's Pork Chop Dinner

Classic Cabbage Rolls

Slow Cooker Recipe

    6 cups water
   12 large cabbage leaves
    1 pound lean ground lamb
   ½ cup cooked rice
    1 teaspoon salt
   ¼ teaspoon dried oregano leaves
   ¼ teaspoon ground nutmeg
   ¼ teaspoon black pepper
  1½ cups tomato sauce

Bring water to a boil in large saucepan. Turn off heat. Soak cabbage leaves in water 5 minutes; remove, drain and cool.

Combine lamb, rice, salt, oregano, nutmeg and pepper in large bowl. Place 2 tablespoonfuls mixture in center of each cabbage leaf; roll firmly. Place cabbage rolls in slow cooker, seam-side down. Pour tomato sauce over cabbage rolls. Cover and cook on Low 8 to 10 hours. *Makes 6 servings*

Food Fact: *Once your dish is cooked, don't keep it in the slow cooker too long. Foods need to be kept cooler than 40°F or hotter than 140°F to avoid the growth of harmful bacteria. Remove food to a clean container, cover and refrigerate as soon as possible. Do not reheat leftovers in the slow cooker. Use a microwave oven, the range-top or the oven for reheating.*

Classic Cabbage Rolls

Spanish-Style Couscous

Slow Cooker Recipe

1 pound lean ground beef
1 can (about 14 ounces) beef broth
1 small green bell pepper, cut into ½-inch pieces
½ cup pimiento-stuffed green olives, sliced
½ medium onion, chopped
2 cloves garlic, minced
1 teaspoon ground cumin
½ teaspoon dried thyme leaves
1⅓ cups water
1 cup uncooked couscous

Heat skillet over high heat until hot. Add beef; cook until browned. Pour off fat. Place broth, bell pepper, olives, onion, garlic, cumin, thyme and beef in slow cooker. Cover and cook on Low 4 hours or until bell pepper is tender.

Bring water to a boil over high heat in small saucepan. Stir in couscous. Cover; remove from heat. Let stand 5 minutes; fluff with fork. Spoon couscous onto plates; top with beef mixture.

Makes 4 servings

Food Fact: *To clean your slow cooker, follow the manufacturer's instructions. To make cleanup even easier, spray with nonstick cooking spray before adding food.*

Spanish-Style Couscous

Turkey and Macaroni

Slow Cooker Recipe

1 teaspoon vegetable oil
1½ pounds ground turkey
2 cans (10¾ ounces each) condensed tomato soup, undiluted
2 cups uncooked macaroni, cooked and drained
1 can (16 ounces) corn, drained
½ cup chopped onion
1 can (4 ounces) sliced mushrooms, drained
2 tablespoons ketchup
1 tablespoon mustard
Salt and black pepper to taste

Heat oil in medium skillet; cook turkey until browned. Transfer mixture to slow cooker. Add remaining ingredients to slow cooker. Stir to blend. Cover and cook on Low 7 to 9 hours or on High 3 to 4 hours. *Makes 4 to 6 servings*

Food Fact: *Always taste the finished dish before serving to adjust seasonings to your preference. Consider adding a dash of the following: salt, pepper, seasoned salt, seasoned herb blends, lemon juice, soy sauce, Worcestershire sauce, flavored vinegar or minced fresh herbs.*

Mile-High Enchilada Pie

Slow Cooker Recipe

5 (6-inch) corn tortillas
1 jar (12 ounces) prepared salsa
1 can (15½ ounces) kidney beans, rinsed and
    drained
1 cup shredded cooked chicken
1 cup shredded Monterey Jack with jalapeño cheese

Prepare foil handles for slow cooker (see below); place in slow cooker. Place 1 tortilla on bottom of slow cooker. Top with small amount of salsa, beans, chicken and cheese. Continue layering using remaining ingredients, ending with 1 tortilla and cheese. Cover and cook on Low 6 to 8 hours or on High 3 to 4 hours. Pull out by foil handles. *Makes 4 servings*

Foil Handles: Tear off three 18×2-inch strips of heavy foil or use regular foil folded to double thickness. Crisscross foil strips in spoke design and place in slow cooker to make lifting of tortilla stack easier.

Mile-High Enchilada Pie

Beef Bourguignon

Slow Cooker Recipe

1 boneless beef sirloin steak, ½ inch thick,
    trimmed and cut into ½-inch pieces
    (about 3 pounds)
½ cup all-purpose flour
4 slices bacon, diced
2 medium carrots, diced
8 small new red potatoes, unpeeled, cut into quarters
8 to 10 mushrooms, sliced
20 to 24 pearl onions
3 cloves garlic, minced
1 bay leaf
1 teaspoon dried marjoram leaves
½ teaspoon dried thyme leaves
½ teaspoon salt
    Black pepper to taste
2½ cups Burgundy wine or beef broth

Coat beef with flour, shaking off excess. Set aside.

Cook bacon in large skillet over medium heat until partially cooked. Add beef; cook until browned. Remove beef and bacon with slotted spoon.

Layer carrots, potatoes, mushrooms, onions, garlic, bay leaf, marjoram, thyme, salt, pepper, beef and bacon mixture and wine in slow cooker. Cover and cook on Low 8 to 9 hours or until beef is tender. Remove and discard bay leaf before serving.

Makes 10 to 12 servings

Beef Bourguignon

3-Cheese Chicken & Noodles

Slow Cooker Recipe

3 cups chopped cooked chicken
1½ cups cottage cheese
1 can (10¾ ounces) condensed cream of chicken soup, undiluted
1 (8-ounce) package wide egg noodles, cooked and drained
1 cup grated Monterey Jack cheese
½ cup chicken broth
½ cup diced celery
½ cup diced onion
½ cup diced green bell pepper
½ cup diced red bell pepper
½ cup grated Parmesan cheese
1 can (4 ounces) sliced mushrooms, drained
2 tablespoons butter, melted
½ teaspoon dried thyme leaves

Combine all ingredients in slow cooker. Stir to coat evenly. Cover and cook on Low 6 to 10 hours or on High 3 to 4 hours.

Makes 6 servings

Food Fact: *Vegetables often take longer to cook than meats. Cut vegetables into small, thin pieces and place them near the bottom or sides of the slow cooker. Pay careful attention to the recipe instructions in order to cut vegetables to the proper size so they will cook in the amount of time given.*

3-Cheese Chicken & Noodles

Steak San Marino

Slow Cooker Recipe

¼ cup all-purpose flour
1 teaspoon salt
½ teaspoon black pepper
4 beef round steaks, about 1 inch thick
1 can (8 ounces) tomato sauce
2 carrots, chopped
½ onion, chopped
1 rib celery, chopped
1 teaspoon dried Italian seasoning
½ teaspoon Worcestershire sauce
1 bay leaf
Hot cooked rice

Combine flour, salt and pepper in small bowl. Dredge each steak in flour mixture. Place in slow cooker. Combine tomato sauce, carrots, onion, celery, Italian seasoning, Worcestershire sauce and bay leaf in small bowl; pour into slow cooker. Cover and cook on Low 8 to 10 hours or on High 4 to 5 hours.

Remove and discard bay leaf. Serve steaks and sauce over rice.

Makes 4 servings

Food Fact: *A good tip to keep in mind while shopping is that you can, and in fact should, use tougher, inexpensive cuts of meat. Top-quality cuts, such as loin chops or filet mignon, fall apart during long cooking periods and therefore are not great choices to use in the slow cooker. Keep those for roasting, broiling or grilling and save money when you use your slow cooker.*

Steak San Marino

Pineapple Chicken and Sweet Potatoes

Slow Cooker Recipe

⅔ cup plus 3 tablespoons all-purpose flour, divided
1 teaspoon salt
1 teaspoon ground nutmeg
½ teaspoon ground cinnamon
⅛ teaspoon onion powder
⅛ teaspoon black pepper
6 chicken breasts
3 sweet potatoes, peeled and sliced
1 can (10¾ ounces) condensed cream of chicken soup, undiluted
½ cup pineapple juice
¼ pound mushrooms, sliced
2 teaspoons brown sugar
½ teaspoon grated orange peel
Hot cooked rice

Combine ⅔ cup flour, salt, nutmeg, cinnamon, onion powder and black pepper in large bowl. Thoroughly coat chicken in flour mixture. Place sweet potatoes on bottom of slow cooker. Top with chicken.

Combine soup, juice, mushrooms, remaining 3 tablespoons flour, sugar and orange peel in small bowl; stir well. Pour soup mixture into slow cooker. Cover and cook on Low 8 to 10 hours or on High 3 to 4 hours. Serve chicken and sauce over rice.

Makes 6 servings

**Pineapple Chicken and
Sweet Potatoes**

Fiesta Rice and Sausage

Slow Cooker Recipe

1 teaspoon vegetable oil
2 pounds spicy Italian sausage, casing
   removed
2 cloves garlic, minced
2 teaspoons ground cumin
4 onions, chopped
4 green bell peppers, chopped
3 jalapeño peppers,* seeded and minced
4 cups beef broth
2 packages (6¼ ounces each) long-grain and wild rice mix

*Jalapeño peppers can sting and irritate the skin; wear rubber gloves when handling peppers and do not touch eyes.

Heat oil in large skillet; add sausage. Break up sausage with back of spoon while cooking; cook until browned, about 5 minutes. Add garlic and cumin; cook 30 seconds. Add onions, bell peppers and jalapeño peppers. Sauté mixture until onions are tender, about 10 minutes. Pour mixture into slow cooker. Stir in beef broth and rice.

Cover and cook on High 1 to 2 hours or on Low 4 to 6 hours.

Makes 10 to 12 servings

Food Fact: *If you do any advance preparation, such as trimming meat or cutting vegetables, make sure you then cover and refrigerate the food until you are ready to start cooking. Store uncooked meats and vegetables separately. If you are preparing meat, poultry or fish, remember to wash your cutting board, utensils and hands with soap and hot water before touching other foods.*

Fiesta Rice and Sausage

Mom's Tuna Casserole

Slow Cooker Recipe

2 cans (12 ounces each) tuna, drained and
    flaked
3 cups diced celery
3 cups crushed potato chips, divided
6 hard-cooked eggs, chopped
1 can (10¾ ounces) condensed cream of mushroom soup,
    undiluted
1 can (10¾ ounces) condensed cream of celery soup,
    undiluted
1 cup mayonnaise
1 teaspoon dried tarragon leaves
1 teaspoon black pepper

Combine all ingredients, except ½ cup potato chips, in slow cooker;
stir well. Top mixture with remaining ½ cup potato chips. Cover
and cook on Low 5 to 8 hours. *Makes 8 servings*

Mom's Tuna Casserole

Cheesy Pork and Potatoes

½ pound ground pork, cooked and crumbled
½ cup finely crushed saltine crackers
⅓ cup barbecue sauce
1 egg
3 tablespoons margarine
1 tablespoon vegetable oil
4 potatoes, peeled and thinly sliced
1 onion, thinly sliced
1 cup grated mozzarella cheese
⅔ cup evaporated milk
1 teaspoon salt
¼ teaspoon paprika
⅛ teaspoon black pepper
   Chopped parsley

Slow Cooker Recipe

Combine pork, crackers, barbecue sauce and egg in large bowl; shape mixture into 6 patties. Heat margarine and oil in medium skillet. Sauté potatoes and onion until lightly browned. Drain and place in slow cooker.

Combine cheese, milk, salt, paprika and pepper in small bowl. Pour into slow cooker. Layer pork patties on top. Cover and cook on Low 3 to 5 hours. Garnish with parsley.   *Makes 6 servings*

Food Fact: *The slow cooker can help you make lower-fat meals because you won't be cooking in fat as you do when you stir-fry and sauté. And tougher, inexpensive cuts of meat have less fat than prime cuts. Many recipes call for trimming excess fat from meat.*

Cheesy Pork and Potatoes

That's Italian Meat Loaf

Slow Cooker Recipe

1 (8-ounce) can tomato sauce, divided
1 egg, lightly beaten
½ cup chopped onion
½ cup chopped green bell pepper
⅓ cup dry seasoned bread crumbs
2 tablespoons grated Parmesan cheese
½ teaspoon garlic powder
¼ teaspoon black pepper
1 pound ground beef
½ pound ground pork or veal
1 cup shredded Asiago cheese

Reserve ⅓ cup tomato sauce; set aside in refrigerator. Combine remaining tomato sauce and egg in large bowl. Stir in onion, bell pepper, bread crumbs, Parmesan cheese, garlic powder and black pepper. Add ground beef and pork; mix well and shape into loaf.

Place meat loaf on foil handles (see page 56). Place in slow cooker. Cover and cook on Low 8 to 10 hours or on High 4 to 6 hours; internal temperature should read 170°F.

Spread meat loaf with reserved tomato sauce. Sprinkle with Asiago cheese. Cover and cook 15 minutes or until cheese is melted. Using foil handles, remove meat loaf from slow cooker.

Makes 8 servings

That's Italian Meat Loaf

Chicken Sausage Pilaf

Slow Cooker Recipe

1 tablespoon vegetable oil
1 pound chicken or turkey sausage, casing
   removed
1 cup uncooked rice and pasta mix
4 cups chicken broth
2 ribs celery, diced
¼ cup slivered almonds
   Salt and black pepper to taste

Heat oil in large skillet; add sausage. Break up sausage with back of spoon while cooking; cook until browned, about 5 minutes. Add rice-pasta mix to skillet. Cook 1 minute. Place mixture in slow cooker. Add remaining ingredients to slow cooker; stir well. Cover and cook on Low 7 to 10 hours or on High 3 to 4 hours or until rice is tender. *Makes 4 servings*

Food Fact: *If you do use fatty cuts of meat, such as sausage or ribs, consider browning them first on top of the range to cook off excess fat before adding them to the slow cooker.*

Chicken Sausage Pilaf

Classic Beef & Noodles

Slow Cooker Recipe

  2 pounds beef stew meat, trimmed and cut
      into cubes
  ¼ pound mushrooms, sliced into halves
  2 tablespoons chopped onion
  2 cloves garlic, minced
  1 teaspoon salt
  1 teaspoon dried oregano leaves
  ½ teaspoon black pepper
  ¼ teaspoon dried marjoram leaves
  1 bay leaf
1½ cups beef broth
  ⅓ cup dry sherry
  1 (8-ounce) container sour cream
  ½ cup all-purpose flour
  ¼ cup water
  4 cups hot cooked noodles

Combine beef, mushrooms, onion, garlic, salt, oregano, pepper, marjoram and bay leaf in slow cooker. Pour in beef broth and sherry. Cover and cook on Low 8 to 10 hours or on High 4 to 5 hours. Remove and discard bay leaf.

If cooking on Low, turn to High. Stir together sour cream, flour and water in small bowl. Stir about 1 cup liquid from slow cooker into sour cream mixture. Stir mixture back into slow cooker. Cover and cook on High 30 minutes or until thickened and bubbly. Serve over noodles. *Makes 8 servings*

Classic Beef & Noodles

The Best of
the Rest

Festive Bacon
& Cheese Dip

Slow Cooker Recipe

2 packages (8 ounces each) cream cheese,
    softened, cut into cubes
4 cups shredded Colby-Jack cheese
1 cup half-and-half
2 tablespoons mustard
1 tablespoon chopped onion
2 teaspoons Worcestershire sauce
½ teaspoon salt
¼ teaspoon hot pepper sauce
1 pound bacon, cooked and crumbled

Place cream cheese, Colby-Jack cheese, half-and-half, mustard,
onion, Worcestershire sauce, salt and pepper sauce in slow cooker.
Cover and cook, stirring occasionally, on Low 1 hour or until cheese
melts. Stir in bacon; adjust seasonings. Serve with crusty bread or
fruit and vegetable dippers. *Makes about 1 quart*

Festive Bacon & Cheese Dip

Oriental Chicken Wings

Slow Cooker Recipe

32 pieces chicken wing drums and flats
1 cup chopped red onion
1 cup soy sauce
¾ cup brown sugar
¼ cup dry sherry
2 tablespoons chopped fresh ginger
2 cloves garlic, minced
Chopped chives

Broil chicken wings, about 5 minutes per side. Transfer chicken to slow cooker.

Stir together onion, soy sauce, brown sugar, sherry, ginger and garlic in large bowl. Add to slow cooker; stir to combine. Cover and cook on Low 5 to 6 hours or on High 2 to 3 hours. Sprinkle with chives. *Makes 32 appetizers*

Food Fact: *Chicken skin tends to shrivel and curl in the slow cooker, so most recipes call for skinless chicken. If you use skin-on pieces, brown them before adding them to the slow cooker.*

Oriental Chicken Wings

Suzie's Sloppy Joes

Slow Cooker Recipe

  3 pounds lean ground beef
  1 cup chopped onion
  3 cloves garlic, minced
1¼ cups ketchup
  1 cup chopped red bell pepper
  5 tablespoons Worcestershire sauce
  4 tablespoons brown sugar
  3 tablespoons vinegar
  3 tablespoons mustard
  2 teaspoons chili powder
    Hamburger buns

Brown ground beef, onion and garlic in large skillet. Drain excess fat.

Combine ketchup, bell pepper, Worcestershire sauce, brown sugar, vinegar, mustard and chili powder in slow cooker. Stir in beef mixture. Cover and cook on Low 6 to 8 hours. Spoon into hamburger buns. *Makes 8 to 10 servings*

BBQ Pork Sandwiches

Slow Cooker Recipe

4 pounds boneless pork loin roast, fat
    trimmed
1 can (14½ ounces) beef broth
⅓ cup FRENCH'S® Worcestershire Sauce
⅓ cup FRANK'S® REDHOT® Sauce

Sauce

½ cup ketchup
½ cup molasses
¼ cup FRENCH'S® CLASSIC YELLOW® Mustard
¼ cup FRENCH'S® Worcestershire Sauce
2 tablespoons FRANK'S® REDHOT® Sauce

1. Place roast on bottom of slow cooker. Combine broth, *⅓ cup each* Worcestershire and REDHOT sauce. Pour over roast. Cover and cook on high-heat setting 5 hours* or until roast is tender.

2. Meanwhile, combine ingredients for sauce in large bowl; set aside.

3. Transfer roast to large cutting board. Discard liquid. Coarsely chop roast. Stir into reserved sauce. Spoon pork mixture on large rolls. Serve with deli potato salad, if desired.

Makes 8 to 10 servings

*Or cook 10 hours on low-heat setting.

BBQ Pork Sandwich

Asparagus and Cheese Side Dish

Slow Cooker Recipe

1½ pounds fresh asparagus, trimmed
2 cups crushed saltine crackers
1 can (10¾ ounces) condensed cream of asparagus soup, undiluted
1 can (10¾ ounces) condensed cream of chicken soup, undiluted
¼ pound American cheese, cut into cubes
⅔ cup slivered almonds
1 egg

Combine all ingredients in large bowl; stir well. Pour into slow cooker. Cover and cook on High 3 to 3½ hours.

Makes 4 to 6 servings

Food Fact: *Manufacturers recommend that slow cookers should be one-half to three-quarters full for best results.*

Asparagus and Cheese Side Dish

Spicy Beans Tex-Mex

Slow Cooker Recipe

⅓ cup lentils
1⅓ cups water
5 strips bacon
1 onion, chopped
1 can (16 ounces) pinto beans, undrained
1 can (16 ounces) red kidney beans, undrained
1 can (15 ounces) diced tomatoes, undrained
3 tablespoons ketchup
3 cloves garlic, minced
1 teaspoon chili powder
½ teaspoon ground cumin
¼ teaspoon red pepper flakes
1 bay leaf

Boil lentils in water 20 to 30 minutes in large saucepan; drain. In small skillet, cook bacon until crisp; remove, drain and crumble bacon. In same skillet, cook onion in bacon drippings until soft. Combine lentils, bacon, onion, beans, tomatoes, ketchup, garlic, chili powder, cumin, pepper flakes and bay leaf in slow cooker. Cook on High 3 to 4 hours. *Makes 8 to 10 servings*

Spicy Beans Tex-Mex

Donna's Potato Casserole

Slow Cooker Recipe

1 can (10¾ ounces) condensed cream of
    chicken soup, undiluted
8 ounces sour cream
¼ cup chopped onion
¼ cup plus 3 tablespoons butter, melted, divided
1 teaspoon salt
2 pounds potatoes, peeled and chopped
2 cups shredded Cheddar cheese
1½ to 2 cups stuffing mix

Combine soup, sour cream, onion, ¼ cup butter and salt in small bowl.

Combine potatoes and cheese in slow cooker. Pour soup mixture into slow cooker; mix well. Sprinkle stuffing mix over potato mixture; drizzle with remaining 3 tablespoons butter. Cover and cook on Low 8 to 10 hours or on High 5 to 6 hours.

Makes 8 to 10 servings

Food Fact: *If you'd like to adapt your own favorite recipe to a slow cooker recipe, you'll need to follow a few guidelines. First, try to find a similar slow cooker recipe in this publication or your manufacturer's guide. Note the cooking times, liquid, quantity and size of meat and vegetable pieces. Because the slow cooker captures moisture, you will want to reduce the amount of liquid, often by as much as half. Add dairy products toward the end of the cooking time so they do not curdle.*

Donna's Potato Casserole

"Peachy Keen" Dessert Treat

1⅓ cups rolled old-fashioned oats
1 cup granulated sugar
1 cup packed brown sugar
⅔ cup buttermilk baking mix
2 teaspoons ground cinnamon
½ teaspoon ground nutmeg
2 pounds fresh peaches (about 8 medium), sliced

Stir together oats, sugars, baking mix, cinnamon and nutmeg in large bowl. Stir in peaches; mix until well blended. Pour mixture into slow cooker. Cover and cook on Low 4 to 6 hours.

Makes 8 to 12 servings

Food Fact: *The benefits of your slow cooker:*

• *No need for constant attention or frequent stirring*

• *No worry about burning or overcooking*

• *No sink full of pots and pans to scrub at the end of a long day*

• *Great for parties and buffets*

• *Keeps your kitchen cool by keeping your oven turned off*

• *Saves energy—cooking on the low setting uses less energy than most light bulbs*

"Peachy Keen" Dessert Treat

Decadent Chocolate Delight

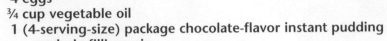

Slow Cooker Recipe

1 package chocolate cake mix
8 ounces sour cream
1 cup chocolate chips
1 cup water
4 eggs
¾ cup vegetable oil
1 (4-serving-size) package chocolate-flavor instant pudding
　　and pie filling mix

Lightly grease inside of slow cooker.

Combine all ingredients in large bowl. Pour into slow cooker. Cover and cook on Low 6 to 8 hours or on High 3 to 4 hours. Serve hot or warm with ice cream.　　　　　　　　　　　*Makes 12 servings*

Decadent Chocolate Delight

Acknowledgments

The publisher would like to thank the companies and organizations listed below for the use of their recipes and photographs in this publication.

A.1.® Steak Sauce

Birds Eye®

Butterball® Turkey Company

Campbell Soup Company

Del Monte Corporation

Hormel Foods Corporation

The HV Company

Kikkoman International Inc.

Lawry's® Foods, Inc.

The Procter & Gamble Company

Reckitt & Colman Inc.

Recipe Index